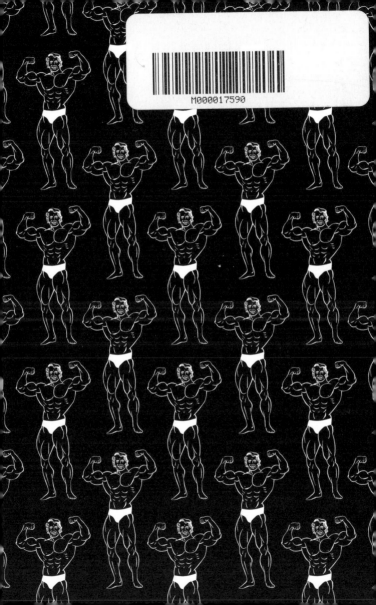

What Would
Arnie Do?

What Would Arnie Do?

Motivate and perspirate with his best quotes

POP PRESS

1 3 5 7 9 10 8 6 4 2

Pop Press, an imprint of Ebury Publishing
20 Vauxhall Bridge Road
London SW1V 2SA

Pop Press is part of the Penguin Random House group of companies
whose addresses can be found at global.penguinrandomhouse.com

Compilation © Pop Press 2019

First published by Pop Press in 2019

www.penguin.co.uk

A CIP catalogue record for this book is available from the British Library

ISBN 9781785038778

Typeset in 23/27 pt Futura Std
by Integra Software Services Pvt. Ltd, Pondicherry

Printed and bound in Great Britain by Clays Ltd, Elcograf S.p.A.

Penguin Random House is committed to a
sustainable future for our business, our readers
and our planet. This book is made from Forest
Stewardship Council® certified paper.

CONTENTS

FITNESS

"Because the mind motivates you to train the body, you have to train the mind first."

"It's simple: if it jiggles, it's fat."

"The best activities for your health are pumping and humping."

"Good bodybuilders have the same mind when it comes to sculpting [that] a sculptor has."

"No lifts, no gifts."

On keeping fit during the holidays.

"If you can change your diet and exercise to give yourself a different body, you can apply the same principles to anything else."

"You look better, which makes you feel better. And when you feel better, you naturally look better."

"Once you realise that life is an athletic event, it follows that you can train for it."

"If you are motivated enough, you will find a way to make sure you get in your training sessions, no matter what."

"The mind-body connection is the same in sex as it is in training. If I tell myself to train the thighs, then the calves, it's boom, boom, mind-thighs, mind-calves, mind-this, mind-that. And it's the same with fucking – mind-cock."

MOTIVATION

"Stop whining."

"The mind is the limit. As long as the mind can envision the fact that you can do something, you can do it, as long as you really believe 100 per cent."

"I always wanted to be an inspiration for people."

"Fitness. Is. For. Everyone."

"What we face may look insurmountable. But I learned something from all those years of training and competing. I learned something from all those sets and reps when I didn't think I could lift another ounce of weight. What I learned is that we are always stronger than we know."

"You can't climb the ladder of success with your hands in your pockets."

"If you don't find the time, if you don't do the work, you don't get the results."

"None of my rules of success will work unless you do."

"You can have results or excuses, but not both."

"*Anything I've ever attempted, I was always willing to fail.*"

PHILOSOPHY

"I don't want to learn anything, and I don't want to become anything. All I want is to go out in the world with a stick, a hat, and a monkey."

The young Arnold on what he wanted to do when he grew up.

"As a kid I always idolised the winning athletes. It is one thing to idolise heroes. It is quite another to visualise yourself in their place. When I saw great people, I said to myself: 'I can be there.'"

"I look down at people who are waiting, who are helpless. I like people who think there is more to life than eating or going to the toilet."

"Strength does not come from winning. Your struggles develop your strengths. When you go through hardships and decide not to surrender, that is strength."

"I am not stopped by risks. Suppose a person takes the risk and fails. Then the person must try again. You cannot fail forever. If you try ten times, you have a better chance of making it on the eleventh try than if you didn't try at all."

"I can apply
my success to
everything. The same
with business. I'm so
determined to make
millions of dollars
that I cannot fail. In
my mind I've already
made the millions;
now it's just a matter
of going through the
motions."

"For me life is continuously being hungry. The meaning of life is not simply to exist, to survive, but to move ahead, to go up, to achieve, to conquer."

"Help others and give something back. I guarantee you will discover that while public service improves the lives and the world around you, its greatest reward is the enrichment and new meaning it will bring your own life."

"Milk is for babies. When you grow up you have to drink beer."

"I don't have any weak points. I had weak points three years ago, but my main thing in mind is, my goal always was, to even everything out to the point … that everything is perfect."

FAME

"Doing battle with a giant mechanical snake left me sore for a week."

The perils of shooting action movies.

"In Hollywood, they said I would never become a leading man. They used to say, 'your body is too big'. Then they said, 'Plus your accent gives me the creeps.'"

"I literally hated having to sleep."

On becoming the biggest star in Hollywood.

"I have a love interest in every one of my films: a gun."

"You can scream at me, call me for a shoot at midnight, keep me waiting for hours – as long as what ends up on the screen is perfect."

"My own dreams fortunately came true in this great state. I became Mr Universe; I became a successful businessman. And even though some people say I still speak with a slight accent, I have reached the top of the acting profession."

"I didn't leave bodybuilding until I felt that I had gone as far as I could go. It will be the same with my film career. When I feel the time is right, I will then consider public service. I feel that the highest honour comes from serving people and your country."

"The very things that they said would make it impossible for me to be successful in acting were the things that became my assets."

"You see stars who have people drive for them, answer calls for them, make dates for them, pick out their clothes for them, pick up their shoes. They have people practically walk and run for them. And then they begin to wonder why they feel ineffective and disconnected."

"*I came to
Hollywood and
within a decade
I was one of the
biggest action stars
of all time.*"

BODYBUILDING

"Bodybuilding is much like any other sport. To be successful, you must dedicate yourself 100 per cent to your training, diet and mental approach."

"Fitness is a right."

"If you told me that if I ate a kilo of shit I would put on muscles, I would eat it."

"I knew in my mind that I was not geared for elegance. I wanted to be massive. It was the difference between cologne and sweat."

"I deserve that pedestal, I own it, and the sea ought to part for me. Just get out of the fucking way, I'm on a mission. So just step aside and gimme the trophy."

Arnie's mind-set before a bodybuilding competition.

"I wanted every single person who touched a weight to equate the feeling of the barbell with my name."

"I get laid on purpose. I can't sleep before competition and I'm up all night, anyway, so instead of staring at the ceiling I figure I might as well find somebody and fuck."

"What's the use of building your body if you don't use it?"

"When you're a
bodybuilder, the gym
is your office."

"In the event of
life, you don't get
another chance ... if
that's not a reason to
stay in shape, I don't
know what is!"

SUCCESS

"The most important rule of all: Work your butt off."

"Sleep faster."

"I love it when someone says that no one has ever done this before, because then when I do it that means that I'm the first one that has done it."

"Be hungry for success, hungry to make your mark, hungry to be seen and to be heard and to have an effect. And as you move up and become successful, make sure also to be hungry for helping others."

"The journey of a thousand miles starts with a single step."

"If I can see it and believe it, then I can achieve it."

"Failure is not an option. Everyone has to succeed."

"The worst thing
I can be is the same
as everybody else.
I hate that."

"I like the colour red because it's a fire. And I see myself as always being on fire."

"The No. 1 lesson of being successful is having a vision. Because when you have a vision of where you want to go in life and what you want to be, then it is just a matter of doing the work to get there."

POLITICS

"*I went from being the Terminator to being the Governator.*"

"My relationship to power and authority is that I'm all for it. People need somebody to watch over them. Ninety-five per cent of the people in the world need to be told what to do and how to behave."

"One of my movies was called True Lies. It's what the Democrats should have called their convention."

"This guy owes me bacon now ... you can't have egg without bacon."

On being pelted with eggs on the campaign trail.

"I have a private plane. But I fly commercial when I go to environmental conferences."

"It was the most difficult decision to make in my entire life, except the one in 1978 when I decided to get a bikini wax."

On deciding to run for office.

"To those critics who are so pessimistic about our economy, I say, 'Don't be economic girlie men!'"

"Failure is no option, it just doesn't exist."

Dealing with the budget crisis.

"Terminate them at the polls."

Arnie's suggestion on what the electorate should do to his opponents.

"He needs to do something about those skinny legs. I'm going to make him do some squats. And then we're going to make him do some biceps curls to beef up those scrawny little arms. But if he could only do something about putting some meat on his ideas."

On Barack Obama.

FILMS

"*I'll be back.*"

The Terminator

"I eat Green Berets for breakfast. And right now, I'm very hungry!"

Commando

"*If you yield only to a conqueror then prepare to be conquered.*"

Red Sonja

"If it bleeds, we can kill it."

Predator

"I hope you leave enough room for my fist because I'm going to ram it into your stomach and break your god-damn spine."

The Running Man

"You're luggage."

Despatching a couple of crocodiles in *Eraser*.

"Consider that a divorce."

After shooting his wife Sharon Stone in *Total Recall*.

"Come with me if you want to live."

Terminator 2

"*You should have cloned yourself ... so you can go fuck yourself!*"

The 6th Day

"Put that cookie down, NOW!"

Jingle All the Way

"Get to the chopper!"

Predator

"Hasta la vista, baby."

Terminator 2

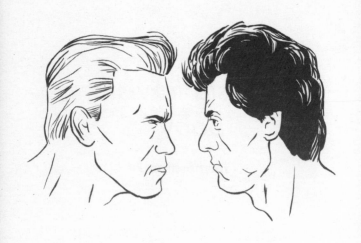

RIVALRY

"I'd be angry at hearing my name mentioned in the same breath as Stallone's. Stallone uses body doubles for some of the close-ups in his movies. I don't."

"Just because a guy can afford to put a Rodin statue in his fucking living room does not mean he is an art historian. Sly is not half as smart as he thinks he is."

"Do you remember the Rambo knife became so big it was like a sword? No one has a knife like that! But Stallone had one built, so I had to come in with a bigger one. This is how it went."

"Everyone in this town is jealous of the next guy. They're all a bunch of jealous bitches sitting around saying, 'I hope he takes a dive.'"

Arnie taking the reviews for *Last Action Hero* on the chin.

"[A] schnitzel up their ass."

His thoughts on his supposed Republican allies.

"When Congress
is less popular
than herpes &
Nickelback, how
do 97 per cent of
them get re-elected?
Gerrymandering."

"President Trump, I just saw your press conference with Putin and it was embarrassing. I mean, you stood there like a little wet noodle, like a little fan boy."

"I mean, what are you going to bring back next? Floppy disks? Fax machines? Beanie Babies? Beepers? Or Blockbuster?"

On Trump's plans for helping the coal industry.

"You should think about hiring a new joke writer and a fact checker."

Twitter response to Trump claiming Arnold was fired from *The Apprentice*.

"*I never mind picking up new titles. Mr Universe, Mr Olympia, Terminator, Governor ... If you want to call me Snowflake, that's fine – it would have been a fantastic Mr Freeze line.*"

WINNING

"I welcome and seek your ideas, but do not bring me small ideas; bring me big ideas to match our future."

"Everybody pities the weak; jealousy you have to earn."

"The resistance that you fight physically in the gym and the resistance that you fight in life can only build a strong character."

"I didn't mind basic training. It taught me that something that seems impossible at the start can be achieved."

"Positive thinking can be contagious. Being surrounded by winners helps you develop into a winner."

"Never do anything that you're not really prepped, overly prepped for. Just like in bodybuilding, don't go in the competition if you haven't done the reps. The same is with anything else."

"*I was always honest about my weak points ... I think it's the key to success in everything.*"

"I consider myself a bottom-line kind of guy. What I'm interested in when I undertake something is results."

"Money doesn't make you happy. I now have $50 million but I was just as happy when I had $48 million."

"I knew I was a winner. I knew I was destined for great things. People will say that kind of thinking is totally immodest. I agree. Modesty is not a word that applies to me in any way – I hope it never will."

Acknowledgements

p16, 38, 40, 54, 67, 115 from Arnold Schwarzenegger, *Total Recall* (2013); p109 from Arnold Schwarzenegger's Facebook; p6, 17, 51, 104, 105, 106, 108 from Arnold Schwarzenegger's Twitter; p8, 9, 10, 59, 66 from Arnold Schwarzenegger and Bill Dobbins, *Arnold's Bodybuilding for Men* (1986); p20, 58, 119 from Arnold Schwarzenegger and Bill Dobbins, *The New Encyclopaedia of Modern Bodybuilding* (1999); p2, 7, 31, 55, 116, 118, 121 from Arnold Schwarzenegger and Douglas Kent Hall, *Arnold: The Education of a Bodybuilder* (1989); p107 from ATTN video (2018); p102 quoted in *Beyond Fest* (2017); p29, 30 from *Boston Globe*, 'Winning According to Schwarzenegger' (1982); p41 quoted in Brad J. Bushman, *Aggression and Violence* (2016); p15 quoted in Brian Payne by *Goal Mapping* (2006); p87 from *Commando* (1985); p46 quoted in *Cosmopolitan*, 'The High Price of Sudden Fame' (1987); p78 quoted in *Daily Beast*, 'Arnold Schwarzenegger Comes Clean' (2012); p45 from *Daily Mail* interview (2015); p103 from *Daily Mail* interview (1993); p43 from *Daily Telegraph*, 'If it's heroes you want look no further than Friedman and Smith' (2003); p83 quoted in *Daily Telegraph*, 'Schwarzenegger Pummels Barack Obama' (2008); p33 quoted in Donald Emmons, *Words for the Journey* (2012); p91 from *Eraser* (1996); p32 quoted in *Esquire*, 'The Wisdom of Arnold Schwarzenegger' (2007); p120 quoted in Francis Tapon, *Life Lessons from Backpacking Across America* (2011); p69 from Gregg Valentino, *Death Drugs and Muscle* (2011); p42, 114 from George Ilian, *50 Life and Business Lessons from Arnold Schwarzenegger* (2016); p47 quoted in *Hollywood Reporter* (2012); p53, 100, 101 quoted in Ian Halperin, *The Governator* (2010); p39, 82 quoted in *iNewspaper* interview (2017); p70 quoted in Jesse Ventura, *Sh*t Politicians Say* (2018); p95 from *Jingle All the Way* (1996); p113 quoted in Manoranjan Kumar, *Dictionary of Quotations* (2008); p27 quoted in *National Observer*, 'Pumping Iron Pumps Up Arnold' (1977); p28 from *New York Sunday News*, 'More Than Just a Beautiful Body' (1976); p11, 56, 57 from *Oui Magazine* interview (1977); p89, 96 from *Predator* (1987); p3, 5, 34, 35 from *Pumping Iron* (1977); p88 from *Red Sonja* (1985); p76, 80 from Republican Convention speech (2001); p44 from Rodney Osborne, *The Parallax* (2014); p81 quoted in *Sacramento Bee* (2003); p68 quoted in Stan Barren, *Wise Words* (2015); p112 from State of the State Address (2005); p77 quoted in *Sun*, 'The Game of Throws' (2013); p93, 97 from *Terminator 2* (1991); p90 from *The Running Man* (1987); p86 from *The Terminator* (1984); p79 from *The Tonight Show* interview (2003); p71, 117 from *The Wall Street Journal*, 'Arnold Schwarzenegger Recalls His Best and Worst Financial Bets' (2018); p94 from *The 6th Day* (2000); p92 from *Total Recall* (1990); p20, 21, 23, 62, 63, 64 from USC Commencement Address (2009); p74 from video to promote *Total Recall* (2012); p50 quoted in Vinesh Sukumaran, *From Behaviour to Wellbeing* (2018); p26, 52 quoted in Wendy Leigh, *Arnold: The Early Years* (2014); p14 from World Economic Forum speech (2018).

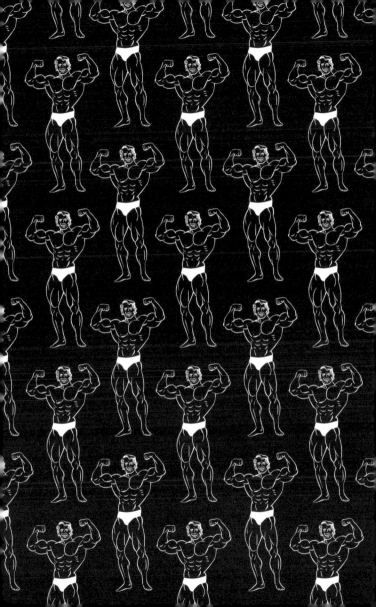